GYMNASTICS SUPERSTAR

SIMONE BILES

GYMN STARS

GymnStars Volume 6

BY CHRISTINE **DZIDRUMS**

GYMNASTICS **SUPERSTAR**

SIMONE BILES

GymnStars Volume 6

Creative **M**edia **P**ublishing

BY CHRISTINE **DZIDRUMS**

CREATIVE MEDIA, INC.
PO Box 6270
Whittier, California 90609-6270
United States of America

www.creativemedia.net

Cover photo by Ricardo Bufolin
Book & cover design by Joseph Dzidrums

First Edition: January 2016

Library of Congress Control Number: 2015920211

ISBN 978-1-938438-42-4   10 9 8 7 6 5 4 3 2 1

For
Every Aspiring Olympian

Table of Contents

*"Don't follow your dreams.
Chase them."*

Five-year-old Simone Biles walked into Bannon's Gymnastix in Houston, Texas. Her big brown eyes danced with excitement and wonder. Just a few feet away, a young girl floated through the air during a dynamic tumbling sequence. Another gymnast resembled an elegant ballerina as she performed a handstand on a balance beam. A third athlete completed a risky release move on the uneven bars.

Gymnastics looked scary. It seemed difficult. Most of all, the sport looked fun!

Simone was on a field trip with her day-care class. She eyed the other gymnasts longingly. How fortunate they were to train at Bannon's.

"I want to try gymnastics," Simone thought. "I can do what they're doing. I just know it."

Finally, the guide finished the tour. Squirming children eyed the gym excitedly.

"Who would like to play on the gym's foam mats?" the worker asked.

"Me!" Simone answered. "I want to try!"

The eager five-year-old sprinted onto the springy mat. The soft, protective surface kept gymnasts safe even during hard falls. Simone began imitating the gymnasts' moves with stunning accuracy. After several minutes, she could execute a few elementary skills.

From across the room, Coach Ronnie studied the young girl in wonderment. Simone was a blast of energy in a tiny package. Furthermore, she possessed what every gymnast desired: natural talent and relentless drive.

"Look at that young girl," Ronnie raved to her coworker, Coach Aimee Boorman. "She's amazing."

"Her talent was evident at a young age," Aimee later told *The Root.* "She knew how to flip."

Both coaches watched Simone with keen interest. The tiny girl was a quick learner. She was also fearless, attempting skill after skill until she succeeded. The women exchanged a knowing look.

A few days later, the young girl's parents, Ronald and Nellie, received a letter from Bannon's Gymnastix. In the note, Aimee and Ronnie praised Simone's tremendous talent and undeterred grit. They had openings in classes at Bannon's. Was their daughter interested in signing up for lessons?

Ronald and Nellie were not gymnastics experts. Like many people, they watched the televised sport every four years at the Olympics, but they didn't know an Amanar vault from a Double twisting Yurchenko. They did know two important things about the sport. Gymnastics could provide a positive outlet for their daughter's enormous energy. Plus, lessons would ensure that Simone would receive proper exercise. If their child wanted to try gymnastics, it was fine with them.

"Simone," her parents called. "We need to discuss something with you."

Their energetic daughter ran into the room in her usual bubbly manner. The young girl flashed her megawatt smile. Then she waited for her parents' question.

"Would you like to take gymnastics lessons?" Ronald and Nellie asked.

Simone's big brown eyes illuminated with excitement. Her heart soared with joy.

"Yes," Simone squealed delightedly. "Yes. Yes. Yes."

Swinging on the Uneven Bars
(Ricardo Bufolin)

"Embrace all the moments because anything can happen."

On March 14, 1997, Simone Arianne Biles was born in Columbus, Ohio. As the third child in the family, she had two older brothers, Ronald and Adam. A few years later, she gained a younger sister named Adria.

> **Simone** *is a popular girl's name, but it is sometimes used as a boy's name. Containing two syllables, it is pronounced* **see-mohn** *or* **sih-MOHN***. Simone is the feminine version of Simon. The name is of Hebrew origin. However, it is a popular name with French people. The meaning of Simone is* '**she who hears**' *or* '**listen**.'

Early in Simone's childhood, her birth mother became unable to care for her and Adria. As a result, both girls moved to Houston, Texas, to live with their grandparents, Ronald and Nellie. When the mature couple officially adopted the sisters, the girls began calling them Dad and Mom.

"We did a formal adoption in a court where we were sworn in as a family," Nellie Biles told *The Root*. "It's a blessing."

Ronald Biles was retired from the Air Force while Nellie worked as a registered nurse. Although the couple also had two teenage boys, they quickly realized that raising girls presented unique challenges.

"I thought my boys were a handful," Ronald laughed when he chatted with the *Houston Chronicle*. "But girls ... trust me: constant drama. Simone has a mind of her own. She has a very strong personality."

Beneath her tough exterior, though, Simone was a sweet child with an enormous heart. She wasn't cruel toward others believing that kindness trumped any other personality trait.

In love with gymnastics, Simone spent many hours at the gym. The unhesitating athlete sometimes trained at home by transforming the Biles house into a makeshift gym. Simone would even practice skills on pieces of furniture. Her bed's mattress doubled as a trampoline. She leaped onto and off couches like they were balance beams or vaults. When she performed a backflip off of her swing set, her parents finally had enough. They bought a family trampoline!

Bounce. Hop. Flip.

Little Simone giggled as the bouncy jumping device shot her high into the air. She reached such great heights on the trampoline that sometimes it almost looked like she could grab a cloud in the sky. Whenever she finally tired of jumping, the youngster performed her favorite element, a somersault.

In 2004, Simone sat next to the family television set and watched the summer Olympics. Athens, Greece, hosted the worldwide event that featured hundreds of athletes competing for medals for their country. The Biles family had great fun cheering on epic showdowns in swimming, track and field, tennis, and other sports.

Ohio State Capitol in Columbus
(Joseph Dzidrums)

When the gymnastics events began, Simone watched with keen interest. The little girl held her breath as the world's best gymnasts strutted their best stuff. Graceful athletes tumbled across sky-blue floors while others performed bold backflips on balance beams. Gymnasts swung elegantly from the uneven bars showing off tricky release moves. Girls raced down a long runway to catapult off a vault that sent them flying through the sky. The elite gymnasts made even challenging tricks look simple. The best routines ended with a difficult dismount and a stuck landing.

The 2004 gymnastics event featured polar opposite superstars. Russia's Svetlana Khorkina danced through her striking routines like a prima ballerina headlining the Bolshoi Ballet. Meanwhile, American Carly Patterson blasted through her programs with powerful tumbling and explosive dismounts. Although Simone liked both girls' styles, she preferred Patterson's because it resembled her own.

The women's all-around competition began on August 19. In the esteemed event, each competitor performs a routine on all four apparatuses: balance beam, floor exercise, uneven bars, and vault. At the event's end, the gymnast with the highest total wins the championship. Thus, the athlete earns the noble title of the best all-around gymnast.

The Athens' all-around featured an unforgettable battle between Khorkina's grace and Patterson's power. Both women were incredible athletes; either could win on any given day. Who would take the gold medal on the evening that mattered most?

Simone held her breath as Carly competed in the epic showdown. The Texan displayed great consistency as she completed four complex routines. Upon nailing her final event, the floor exercise, the teenager burst into tears of joy. She had completed her programs to the best of her ability. Was it enough? When the scoreboard announced her first place finish, an ecstatic Carly sobbed in disbelief. She became the first American woman to win the all-around at a fully attended Olympics.

Overwhelming emotions flooded seven-year-old Simone as she watched the American celebrate a momentous achievement. Carly smiled proudly during the medal ceremony. As "The Star-Spangled Banner" played, the teenager sang along softly while the gold medal hung from her tiny shoulders.

Simone practically trembled with excitement. She suddenly felt determined and eager. Most of all, Simone Biles felt so inspired by Carly's victory that she hoped to one day compete on the United States gymnastics team.

Vaulting to Victory
(Ricardo Bufolin)

"[Gymnastics] takes a lot of hard work, confidence, and patience. There are lots of little steps involved."

As the years passed, Simone fell deeper in love with gymnastics. Six days a week, she slipped on a leotard for a new lesson. A thoughtful listener and a hard worker, the athlete quickly blossomed into one of America's top junior gymnasts.

Despite her gymnastics success, Nellie and Ronnie insisted that their daughter kept a solid grade point average. In the future, Simone might earn a full college scholarship if she maintained good school marks. The youngster agreed with her parents' rule. After all, she dreamed of one day competing at either UCLA or the University of Alabama.

When Simone wasn't training or studying, she enjoyed family outings, like going to the movies. One afternoon the Biles saw _Stick It_, a movie centered on a rebellious gymnast who shakes up the gymnastics world. Nine-year-old Simone and her sister memorized all of the script's lines.

In summer 2008, another Olympics arrived. This time around, Beijing, China, hosted the celebrated event. As usual, Simone loved the gymnastics competitions best. In a riveting team event, home country favorites, China, won the gold to the delight of the crowd. American powerhouses Nastia Liukin and Shawn Johnson led the United States women to a silver medal while the Russians finished in third place.

Several days later, teammates and friendly rivals, Nastia and Shawn faced off in the highly-anticipated all-around competition. In stark contrast to the 2004 Olympics, the more artistic gymnast prevailed in China. Boasting classical lines reminiscent of a ballerina, Nastia grabbed the podium's top spot, while the athletic-looking Shawn settled for silver. By the end of the games, Nastia had collected a staggering five medals in all. Meanwhile, Shawn had amassed three second-place finishes and a victory on the balance beam.

Although Simone admired both gymnasts, she felt a stronger connection to Shawn. The two girls' bodies looked similar. Both athletes had short, muscular builds that resulted in powerful, fiery gymnastics. Simone could watch Shawn tumble for hours. In fact, she did! The youngster often played Shawn's Olympic routines for inspiration, especially after a rough training day.

Due to age restrictions, Simone was too young to compete at the 2012 Olympics in London, England. She would be eligible to compete in 2016, though. So the focused athlete kept that date in her mind nearly every day.

Just as Simone's gymnastics career built top speed, she began high school. To ensure that the teenager wouldn't feel overwhelmed, her parents enrolled her in a homeschool program. The conscientious decision gave the athlete added flexibility with her school and gymnastics schedule.

Although Simone had stopped attending school in a traditional setting, she still studied hard. In fact, the attentive student looked forward to history class more than any other subject. Historical figures and their lasting influence fascinated her. Too bad algebra didn't have the same effect on her. The gifted gymnast didn't like math in any form!

Sometimes when Simone studied, she caught sight of her petite hands. Their appearance screamed years of gymnastics. Due to the friction of gripping the uneven bars, her weathered skin sported calluses and blisters. She jokingly nicknamed them reptile hands.

On a few occasions, Simone let her sharp mind drift toward thoughts of boys. She liked funny, athletic and thoughtful guys! As far as celebrity crushes went, she sighed over singers Austin Mahone and Zayn Malik. However, actor Zac Efron starred in most of her daydreams. She had watched his comedy, *17 Again*, many times.

In July of 2011, the Biles family boarded a plane bound for Chicago, Illinois. Simone had earned the opportunity to compete in her first major gymnastics competition, the CoverGirl Classic. It marked the biggest event of her fourteen-year-old life.

In the end, Simone had a somewhat underwhelming competition. She placed 20th in the all-around competition. Her highest individual placements happened on the vault and floor exercise, where she placed 5th on both.

While at the event, Simone met a fellow competitor named Katelyn Ohashi. The sociable gymnasts clicked immediately and became fast friends. They remained close long after the competition ended and nicknamed themselves: Double Trouble. It felt good to meet people who loved gymnastics as much as she did.

"We're really good friends." Simone once remarked. "I love her."

Much to Simone's delight, she also began attending camp at the Karolyi Ranch. Romanian husband and wife team Bela and Martha Karolyi trained nine Olympic champions during their coaching career, including Nadia Comaneci, Mary Lou Retton, and Keri Strug. When the dynamic duo retired from coaching in the late 1990s, Marta began working as national team coordinator for USA Gymnastics. She and Bela ran a camp from their home nestled in Texas' Sam Houston National Forest. America's best gymnasts assembled at camp every few months to participate in mock competitions designed to build healthy competitiveness among its athletes.

Thanks to her bubbly personality and friendly demeanor, Simone forged friendships with several other gymnasts. She formed sisterly bonds with Lexie Priessman, Elizabeth Price, and McKayla Maroney.

When the gymnasts weren't training, they relaxed by watching television. On particularly productive days, the girls recorded music videos or short films. If it weren't for the challenging training sessions, gymnastics camp would seem like a weeklong slumber party!

Simone had initially felt intimidated upon arriving at her first camp. Many of the girls there were her idols. They had competed at the world championships or even the Olympics. What was she doing there?

However, the longer she attended camp, the more she relaxed and believed in her abilities. One day, a gymnast that she'd seen on television many times approached her.

"You're great on the floor exercise," the world champion raved. "I wish I could tumble like you."

Stunned by the revelation, Simone's jaw nearly dropped in disbelief. She quickly squeaked out a thank you. The friendly gymnast simply smiled in response and then walked away.

Afterward, Simone replayed the encounter in her mind over and over. Not only had a world competitor noticed her; she had praised her skills. Simone Biles had officially arrived on the radar of USA gymnastics.

Golden Girl
(Ricardo Bufolin)

"Gymnastics is hard."

Simone wasn't the only athlete in her family. Her sister Adria was also a talented gymnast who aspired to compete at the college level. The siblings provided unconditional support to one another as they trained side by side.

After a long day, Simone and Adria tossed on warm pajamas and watched television shows, like *Make It or Break It*, a teen drama about competitive gymnasts. Truthfully, the sisters found the series depiction of elite gymnastics unrealistic, so they often giggled at the show's inaccuracies.

ABC Family's *Pretty Little Liars* held the honor of being Simone's favorite television series. The highly-rated drama centered on four young women attempting to solve their friend's murder. She liked the characters Aria and Hanna best.

Whenever the sisters felt like laughing, they turned on the movie comedy *Mean Girls*. Other times they looked to comedian Adam Sandler for laughter. Simone regarded *Grownups 2* as the funniest movie ever. She also enjoyed his romantic comedy with Jennifer Aniston called *Just Go with It*.

Like many teenagers, the Biles sisters were avid *Hunger Games* fans. The best-selling book series turned movie franchise featured heroine Katniss Everdeen fighting to survive in a dystopic universe. Simone's admired Katniss' portrayal, Jennifer Lawrence, for her big heart and down-to-earth demeanor.

Like so many people, Simone counted herself as a big Disney fan. She loved the animated film *Frozen*, especially the comical scenes with Olaf the snowman. However, Ariel from *The Little Mermaid* remained her all-time favorite animated character.

Sometimes Simone snacked in front of the television by nibbling on a chocolate chip cookie or cookies-n-crème ice cream. Mostly, the athlete chose healthier foods, like carrots, grapes, or pomegranates.

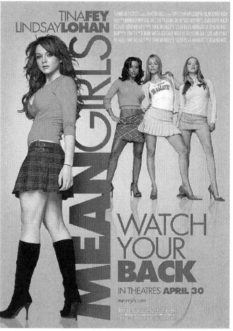

In the summer of 2012, the Olympics ruled the Biles television set once more. The family spent many hours enjoying the London games. Among the highlights, American swimmer Michael Phelps became the most decorated Olympian ever with 22 medals, while Jamaican sprinter Usain Bolt captured hearts with his three gold medals.

On the gymnastics scene, a commanding USA seized gold in the women's team event.

The gifted girls became known as The Fierce Five. Gabby Douglas, McKayla Maroney, Aly Raisman, Kyla Ross, and Jordyn Wieber composed the iconic team.

The Fierce Five were equally dangerous in the individual events. Sixteen-year-old Gabby Douglas' all-around gold marked the third straight American victory in that event. Furthermore, McKayla Maroney captured silver in the vault finals, and team captain Aly Raisman scored two individual medals, including floor exercise gold.

Simone admired all of the Fierce Five members. McKayla's textbook vault technique amazed her while Aly Raisman's difficult floor exercise skills thrilled her. She dreamed of owning Jordyn Wieber's consistency mixed with the fluidity of Gabby Douglas.

Focused Athlete
(Ricardo Bufolin)

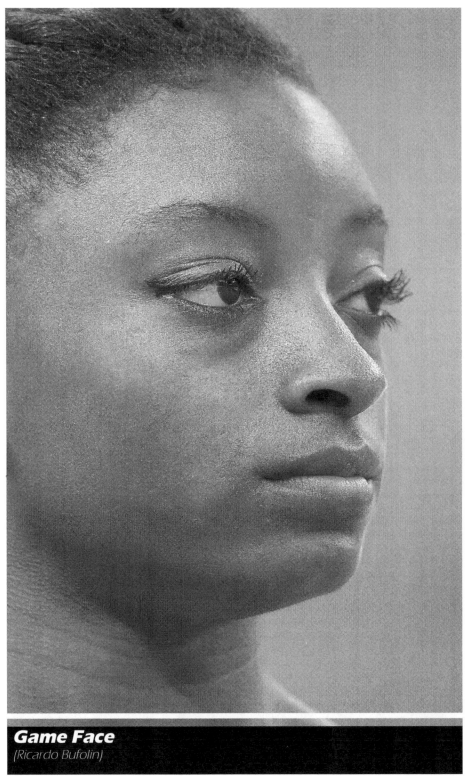

Game Face
(Ricardo Bufolin)

However, Simone admired Kyla Ross above all other Fierce Five members. A steady competitor with elegant, clean lines. Kyla showed remarkable composure even in nerve-wracking circumstances. Simone observed the Southern California teenager carefully hoping to emulate Kyla's strength under pressure.

Simone's favorite gymnasts extended past the American team as well. She admired Romania's Larisa Iordache for her strength in every event. The youngster also held Canadian Victoria Moors' tumbling in high regard, and she loved the breathtaking artistry of Aliya Mustafina.

Simone also liked men's gymnastics. She watched in amazement whenever male athletes performed powerful vaults. If only she could vault alongside the world's best men!

When the year ended, Simone celebrated turning 16 by earning her driver's license. The teenager felt giddy with excitement, especially when her parents gave her the keys to a new Ford Focus. Although truthfully, the gymnast secretly desired a Mercedes-Benz G-Class!

The hungry competitor also advanced to the senior level. At last, she would compete against the best gymnasts from all over the world.

And she could hardly wait.

"Every year I try to upgrade, stay consistent and have fun."

A typical day for Simone Biles always began with her rising with the sun. The dynamic athlete loved breakfast food. Sometimes Simone ate pancakes, bacon, and eggs. On most mornings, she polished off a bowl of Cinnamon Crunch, or Special K cereal, with yogurts and berries.

When Simone arrived at the gym every day, her coach Aimee Boorman waited for her. A supportive coach stands behind almost every great athlete. Aimee was no exception. She was a constant presence in her student's life having guided Simone since she began gymnastics lessons at age five. Although the two worked hard every day, they had fun, too.

"She's playful," Coach Aimee shared. "The other day she said something so funny during practice that I didn't have a comeback for it. She's someone all the other kids want to be around."

Before the beginning of the 2013 season, Simone felt somewhat anxious. Although it thrilled her to compete in the senior ranks, it worried her, too.

"I'm a little nervous, but I'm excited," she admitted. "My goal this year would be making the 2013 worlds team and hopefully doing all-around there."

In March 2013, Simone received her first international assignment, the AT&T American Cup. The excited youngster had grown up watching the televised event. Soon she would travel to Worcester, Massachusetts, to partake in the competition.

"It's exciting and an honor to represent Team USA," she remarked. "This is my first international meet."

"I never thought I'd make it this far," Simone added, in disbelief. "I was just a little girl trying stuff at my house, and then they just put me in gymnastics. I never thought I'd be this good."

On the first day of the American Cup, Simone wore a fuchsia-colored leotard that looked striking against her beautiful dark skin. Standing backstage, she exhaled slowly and then walked into the arena.

Television cameras and a large crowd filled the building. When Simone glanced toward the stands, she saw Fierce Five members Gabby Douglas and Aly Raisman sitting among the spectators.

Sensing her student's distracted state, Coach Aimee quickly helped Simone regroup. She reminded her student to concentrate on the meet, not the crowd. Any loss of concentration in gymnastics could cause severe injury to an athlete.

Simone started the competition strongly on her least-favorite apparatus, the uneven bars. The competitor moved to floor exercise next and delivered a crowd-pleasing routine. On vault, she launched herself high into the air with great form and earned the competition's highest score, 15.733.

"She does not just jump off the table; she explodes," 1984 Olympic Champion Tim Daggett raved.

With three solid routines, Simone would win the entire competition if she nailed her remaining event. The sixteen-year-old suddenly looked overwhelmed. Doubts clouded her mind; She eyed the balance beam anxiously.

Moments later Simone mounted the apparatus and promptly made a tiny bobble. Then she lost her concentration and committed another mistake! When Simone attempted a difficult tumbling pass, she missed the beam and fell to the floor. In a split second, her dream of winning the American Cup disintegrated. What had just happened?

The crowd sensed Simone's disappointment. They joined forces and cheered loudly to encourage her. Buoyed by their support, the teenager jumped back on the apparatus and bravely completed her routine.

"The skills are there," Nastia Liukin remarked on NBC's broadcast. "It's the just the consistency and confidence [missing] that comes with experience."

When the American Cup concluded, Simone finished second in the all-around. She smiled upon hearing that her good buddy, Katelyn Ohashi, won the gold medal. If Simone couldn't win, she felt happy to lose to her friend.

After the medal ceremony, reporters gathered around Simone. They fired numerous questions at her. Many asked if she was aiming for the 2016 Olympics in Rio de Janeiro, Brazil.

"I'm taking it year by year," Simone confessed. "It is still in the back of my mind, and I do think about it."

After winning the silver medal, Simone traveled to Italy for the City of Jesolo Trophy. The teenager performed nearly flawlessly in Europe and led the United States to a team triumph. Simone also won the all-around, vault, balance beam, and floor exercise titles! In all, she left Italy with five gold medals!

Afterward, Team USA flew to Germany for another competition. Once again, Simone scooped up five medals. Things were looking up!

Two months later, Simone arrived in Chicago, Illinois, for the U.S. Classic. Most expected her to win easily, but doubts surrounded her once more. As a result, the anxious gymnast struggled mightily throughout the event and withdrew with one event remaining.

Simone felt overwhelmed and confused. No matter how hard the athlete trained, she struggled with consistency. How could she stop her mind from wandering during events?

After the competition had ended, Marta Karolyi summoned Simone for a meeting. A slight woman with a big voice, the Romanian had a legendary, no-nonsense attitude. The teenager wondered if USA Gymnastics' national team coordinator was upset with her poor performance. She need not have worried.

"I believe in you," Marta said kindly. "Turn the page."

Marta's encouraging words comforted Simone. The team coordinator had faith in her. With just a few words, she urged her to let go of the imperfect competition and keep a fresh attitude for the rest of the season. The pep talk gave the teen an extra shot of confidence.

Suddenly, Simone felt calm. Everything would be okay. She would find a way to regain her confidence and learn to compete more consistently.

Meanwhile, Coach Aimee had another suggestion to help her student. She recommended that Simone work with a sports psychiatrist, a doctor that helps athletes regain focus and confidence. The teenager agreed to meet with Doctor Robert

B. Andrews, a top sports psychiatrist who had helped many athletes reach their competitive best. A former football player, Dr. Andrews understood the stress associated with competition. Under his guidance, the resolute gymnast learned ways to remain calm and focused during competitions.

In mid-August, Simone packed her bags for the all-important U.S. Championships. If she did well, USA Gymnastics would send her to the World Championships in Antwerp, Belgium. As Simone sat calmly on a plane bound for Connecticut, she had never felt more prepared for a competition. It was time to make her dreams come true.

Marta Karolyi
(Ricardo Bufolin)

"The floor exercise is a way to express your personality."

On August 15, 2013, Simone entered the XL Center in Hartford, Connecticut. The petite gymnast wore a blue leotard in size children's large. At the end of P&G's U.S. Championships, one woman would be crowned America's best gymnast. Fierce Five member Kyla Ross was favored to snag the title, but Simone harbored a newfound confidence. She wanted to win and believed she could do it.

On day one of the competition, Simone delivered strong routines on all four events. Both the uneven bars and balance beam went extremely well. She even showed such confidence during her floor routine that it inspired the crowd to clap along to her music. The determined teen ended the night on vault where she delivered an Amanar so enormous that it drew gasps from the crowd.

After day one had concluded, Simone glanced at the scoreboard and did a double take. She couldn't believe it. She was in first place! Her score, 60.500, put her almost one full point over her idol, Kyla Ross.

The following day brought the ultimate test. Would Dr. Andrews' tools help her control her nerves? Could she hold on to first place and win the title of America's number one gymnast?

On the second day of the championships, Simone wore GK's Patriotic Design leotard, a red, white and blue creation that showed off her American pride. Coach Aimee cautioned her pupil to remain focused by thinking of only one apparatus at a time.

"Whatever happens, happens," Simone told herself. "We're all phenomenal gymnasts out here."

Simone began night two on the balance beam. Although the competitor looked shaky on two early elements, she fought hard and remained on the apparatus. Nearly two minutes later, Simone finished the beam without any significant errors. When she walked off the floor, her pleased coach waited for her.

"Good start," Aimee smiled encouragingly. "You got that out of the way."

Simone performed the floor exercise next. On her first tumbling pass, she flew out of bounds. Was it happening again? Would the teenager wilt under pressure once more? No way. She attacked the rest of her program and finished with a gigantic, clean tumbling pass.

With just two programs left in the event, Simone faced the vault next. She felt confident because it was her best event. Sure enough, the assured athlete soared to great heights and earned a 15.8 score. Television cameras caught her parents watching proudly from the stands.

In her final event of the competition, the uneven bars, Simone experienced a slight blunder on her handstand, but she refused to let it unnerve her. She completed the remainder of the routine without any other mistakes.

Biles Airlines
(Ricardo Bufolin)

The sixteen-year-old smiled upon finishing the competition. She stood by Aimee's side and waited for the judges' marks. Had she done well enough to win?

Yes!

When the arena scoreboard was updated, Simone stood atop the standings. She was the winner. Simone Biles was America's number one gymnast!

The Biles' family applauded heartily for their loved one. Adria wept softly and wiped away fallen tears. Ronald and Nellie clapped until their hands ached.

"It's a great feeling to have a champion," her father said choking up with tears. "My entire family is very proud of her."

"It feels good," Simone told *NBC* afterward. "We're all best friends. I was happy for everyone."

Simone had two months of preparations for the World Championships in Belgium. When she returned to Bannon's Gymnastix, a sign on their wall commemorated her national championship. Then she began preparing for the biggest international competition of her life.

Dealing with the stress of high stakes competition can rattle even the most grounded athlete. That's why Simone felt grateful for having a close family. An active household, the Biles often took trips to the beach. Simone loved the scent of the beach's crisp ocean air. Its relaxed atmosphere soothed her. On some occasions, she and Adria even performed gymnastics tricks on the sand.

Sometimes after a fun outing, the family ate at a favorite restaurant. The Biles often alternated which member could select a restaurant. On her turn, Simone usually chose The Olive

Garden. She loved the restaurant's Italian dishes. If only waiters would stop offering her the children's menu!

Before long autumn arrived to signal that it was time for Simone to travel to Belgium for the 2013 World Championships. That year's event did not host a team competition. Instead, gymnasts would compete for all-around and individual event medals.

In the qualifying event, Simone made history on the floor exercise. On her second tumbling pass, she became the first gymnast to land the daring double layout half out in a competition. The FIG (*Fédération Internationale de Gymnastique* or International Federation of Gymnastics) responded by renaming the move: The Biles.

On October 4th, Simone began her quest for the world all-around title. Strangely enough, her biggest obstacle to the gold medal came from idol and teammate Kyla Ross. When media representatives asked questions about their showdown, both athletes focused on their friendship instead.

"We're super best friends," Simone told reporters. "Kyla has a great personality. We laugh the whole time we're together."

Simone started the all-around event sharply. She completed three great routines in a row. Kyla Ross was even stronger, though, and held the lead heading into the final apparatus. It would be a well-fought battle for the gold medal.

Fortunately for Simone, the competition ended with floor exercise. The rookie senior unleashed eye-popping tumbling in a crowd-pleasing routine. In her second tumbling run, the audience roared when she completed the Biles. Throughout the entire program, Simone could not stop smiling. Nerves? What nerves? She was having a blast and loved sharing her enthusiasm with everyone. When the final note of her music ended, the crowd showered her with cheers and whistles of approval.

"I just think she lights up the whole building," 1984 Olympic gold medalist Bart Connor raved.

Simone walked off the floor and gave Aimee a big hug. Then she exchanged a warm embrace with Kyla. Both gymnasts had performed extraordinarily well and would likely finish first and second in the standings

Simone stood on the sidelines next to Kyla. She waited patiently for the posting of her final placement. When the scoreboard flashed the ultimate results, Simone's name reigned in the top position. She had done it. She was world all-around champion.

"She was a kid yesterday, and now she is the best gymnast in the world," exclaimed NBC commentator Tim Daggett.

That's right. Simone Biles was now world all-around champion. She had joined an exclusive club with prominent members. Nadia Comaneci, Shannon Miller, and Shawn Johnson were just a few legends who had also won the world title.

"It feels pretty good," the winner said afterward. "It hasn't sunken in yet, but I know what I've done is a big accomplishment."

Moments later, Simone stood on the top step of the podium at the world championships. A shiny gold medal hung around her neck. She exchanged excited smiles with Kyla, the silver medalist, and bronze winner Aliya Mustafina from Russia. Then she watched the American flag rise while "The Star Spangled Banner" played proudly.

Captivating the Crowd
(Ricardo Bufolin)

"Marta told me once that I should have my own airline."

What's harder than winning a big title? Defending one. Many talented competitors have buckled under the weight of heavy expectations.

Not Simone.

In 2014, the world champion made winning look simple. Armed with brand-new confidence, the focused athlete competed even better than she had the previous year. The result? She won every all-around championship she entered.

Simone arrived at the 2014 U.S. Gymnastics Championships with great fanfare. After all, she was the sport's new face. Her image adorned numerous posters and gigantic billboards around the host city, Pittsburgh, Pennsylvania.

Simone simply shrugged off the attention. Maybe the pressure would have unnerved her over a year ago, but she was a different competitor now. To drive home the point, Simone won the competition by over four points! She also snagged two additional gold medals, on the floor and vault, and scored silver hardware on the balance beam.

A few months later, at the 2014 World Championships in China, the women began the competition with the team event. Simone, Kyla Ross, MyKayla Skinner, Ashton Locklear and Madison Kocian composed Team USA. To say the Americans dominated the competition would be an understatement. Team USA scored a hefty 179.80. The enormously high score propelled them to a massive six-point victory over the second-place finisher China. Meanwhile, Team Russia finished third nearly 8 points behind the Americans.

A few days later, Simone competed in the world all-around competition. The confident gymnast grabbed first place in the first round and never let go of it. When her floor exercise ended, she became the first gymnast to win back-to-back titles since Shannon Miller.

"I just tried to have fun," the two-time all-around champion grinned afterward.

Moments later, Simone stood on the podium during the medal ceremony clutching a floral bouquet. Suddenly, Romania's Larisa Iordache, the silver medalist, peered closely at Simone's flowers. Her eyes grew wide with panic.

"There's a bee in your bouquet," Larisa whispered.

Simone shrieked in fright. She didn't like insects! The teenager tried to swat the bee away, but it wouldn't budge. So, she jumped off the podium and ran around in circles to escape the bee. It didn't work. Fed up, Simone threw her bouquet at the flying insect and began giggling at the absurd situation. After the bee finally flew away, Simone, Larisa and bronze medalist Kyla Ross struggled to stop laughing as they posed for the competition's official photograph.

After the medal ceremony, reporters waited for the two-time world all-around champion. Simone shook her head in disbelief when the press congratulated her on the momentous accomplishment.

Dodging a Bee!
(Ricardo Bufolin)

"It blows my mind," she told a journalist. "It's really weird but it's cool."

After winning back-to-back world championships, Simone Biles became the undisputed star of women's gymnastics. Mary Lou Retton, the 1984 Olympic all-around champion, called her, "unbeatable" and the most talented gymnast she had ever seen. Competitors idolized her. Companies begged the gymnast to pitch their products.

Despite all the new attention Simone remained her usual down-to-earth self. The superstar athlete did not consider herself a celebrity. Besides, she still acted like an average teenager. For instance, the seventeen-year-old spent a lot of time on social media dividing her time between *Twitter, Instagram,* and *Snapchat.* If she got bored with those options, she played *Flappy Bird* on her iPhone.

Music also influenced Simone's life. Although she liked hip hop and top 40 music, country music ruled her heart. Carrie Underwood was her favorite singer. Meanwhile, she listened all the time to Demi Lovato's "Made in the U.S.A,." a patriotic song about an empowered woman declaring her love for her man. Sometimes she found herself humming Tori Kelly's "Dear No One," a tune about an independent girl singing to her future boyfriend.

Despite her passion for music, Simone wasn't about to trade in her leotard for a microphone. In fact, the teen insisted she was a terrible singer. She often joked that her singing sounded like a dying whale.

Whenever Simone craved quality time with her friends, they visited a bowling alley or went shopping at The Galleria. A clothes addict, Simone's could spend hours inside Forever 21. She also loved Bath and Body Works' perfume, Forever Red.

The 2015 gymnastics season began in February with the American Cup. That year also marked the return of two Olympic champions. The 2012 all-around winner Gabby Douglas began a second Olympic bid, while fellow Fierce Five member, Aly Raisman, also hoped to book a ticket to Rio.

When the Olympics champions attended camp for the first time, Gabby and Simone were assigned as roommates. The gymnasts hit it off instantly feeling like they had known each other for years. Some nights they stayed awake talking and laughing so loudly that other gymnasts would bang on the dividing wall just to shush them!

Simone arrived in Indiana, Indianapolis, in June 2015 for her third senior U.S. championship. A victory would make her the first gymnast since Kim Zmeskal to win three straight national titles. To achieve this dream, she needed to defeat friends and heroes, like Gabby Douglas, Kyla Ross, and Aly Raisman.

At the end of two exhausting days, Simone accomplished what few gymnasts have managed by winning her third-straight national title. Minnesota's Maggie Nicholls won the silver; Aly Raisman took the bronze medal, and Gabby Douglas placed fourth.

"Just to have my name behind Kim's is amazing," Simone gushed. "I keep shocking myself."

At the 2015 World Championships in Glasgow, Scotland, Simone led the United States to another team gold medal. Their triumph marked the fourth-straight victory for the Americans in the team event. Their margin of victory? Four plus points ahead of China, the silver medalists.

"We started off with a bang and ended with a bang," Simone smiled.

Two days later, all eyes focused on Simone during the all-around event. If she won the competition, she would become the first female gymnast in history to win three straight all-around titles. Once upon a time, Simone might have crumbled under the intense scenario. Not anymore.

Flashing high-flying gymnastics and unparalleled difficulty, Simone captured a third all-around gold medal. As a matter of fact, the gutsy Texan won the meet by a full point over second place finisher Gabby Douglas. Romania's Larisa Iordache rounded out the podium in third place.

"I keep blowing my own mind," Simone told reporters. "If I could crawl out of my skin and see it, it would be really amazing."

Not so fast, though! Simone wasn't done setting records. In the event finals, she snatched three more medals by finishing third on the vault and first on floor exercise and balance beam. Her 14 medals set a new American record for most hardware won at the world championships.

After her historic achievements, Simone turned professional. She could begin accepting prize money and appearance fees. The decision made her ineligible to compete on any future NCAA teams. Not to worry, though. She still planned to attend college, but now she would pay her way, thanks to deals with Nike and GK Elite.

With her name cemented in gymnastics' history books, Simone had become a hero to many people. Strangers often stopped her in public to request a picture or autograph. At various competitions, fans clutched magazine covers with Simone's image splashed on them begging her to sign them

Simone made sure to thank her fans for supporting her. As always, the thoughtful gymnast was gracious to everyone she encountered. She was a role model now and enjoyed stressing the importance of kindness.

"There is always a little girl in the stands that wants to be just like you," Simone once said. "Don't disappoint her."

"You're my idol," an aspiring gymnast stammered after a competition. "Can I have your autograph?"

Simone's eyes danced with excitement and wonder, just as they had that day she walked into a gym for the first time at age five. The gymnastics superstar was a hero to little girls everywhere. She would not let them down.

"I would love to," Simone smiled.

World Champion Smile
(Ricardo Bufolin)

Competitive Record

2015 World Championships
Team: 1, All Around: 1, Vault: 3, Balance Beam:1, Floor Exercise: 1

2015 U.S. Championships
All Around: 1, Vault: 1, Balance Beam: 1, Floor Exercise: 1

2015 U.S. Classic
All Around: 1, Vault: 1, Balance Beam: 1, Floor Exercise: 1

2015 City of Jesolo Trophy
Team: 1, All Around: 1, Vault: 1, Balance Beam: 1, Floor Exercise: 1

2015 American Cup
All Around: 1

2014 World Championships
Team: 1, All Around: 1, Vault: 2, Balance Beam: 1, Floor Exercise: 1

2014 U.S. Championships
All Around: 1, Vault: 1, Balance Beam: 2, Floor Exercise: 1

2014 U.S. Classic
All Around: 1, Vault: 1, Balance Beam: 1, Floor Exercise: 1

2013 World Championships
All Around: 1, Vault: 2, Balance Beam: 3, Floor Exercise: 1

2013 U.S. Championships
All Around: 1, Vault: 2, Uneven Bars: 2, Balance Beam: 2, Floor Exercise: 2

2013 City of Jesolo Trophy
Team: 1, All Around: 1, Vault: 1, Balance Beam: 1, Floor Exercise: 1

2013 American Cup
All Around: 2

2012 U.S. Championships (Junior)
All-Around: 3, Vault: 1

2012 U.S. Classic (Junior)
All Around: 1, Vault: 1, Floor Exercise: 2

2011 U.S. Championships (Junior)
All-Around: 14, Vault: 7, Balance Beam: 10

Essential Simone Links

Simone's Official Web Page
www.gym-style.com/simonebiles

Simone's Official Twitter Account
www.twitter.com/Simone_Biles

Simone's Official Facebook Page
www.facebook.com/simonebiles

Simone's Instagram
www.instagram.com/simonebiles

Simone's Phhhoto Site
phhhoto.com/simonebiles

USA Gymnastics Home Page
www.usagym.org/pages/index.html

Rio 2016 Olympic Games
www.rio2016.com

Simone's Talent Representation Agency
www.octagon.com

Author Page
www.christinedzidrums.com

About the Author

Christine Dzidrums has written biographies on many inspiring personalities: *Clayton Kershaw, Mike Trout, Yuna Kim, Shawn Johnson, Nastia Liukin, The Fierce Five, Gabby Douglas, Sutton Foster, Kelly Clarkson, Idina Menzel* and *Missy Franklin*. Christine's first Young Adult novel, *Cutters Don't Cry*, won a Moonbeam Children's Book Award. Her follow-up to *Cutters*, *Kaylee: The "What If?" Game*, won a gold medal at the Children's Literary Classic Awards. She also wrote the tween book *Fair Youth* and the beginning reader books *Future Presidents Club* and the *Princess Dessabelle* series. Ms. Dzidrums lives in Southern California with her husband and three children.

www.ChristineDzidrums.com
@ChristineWriter.

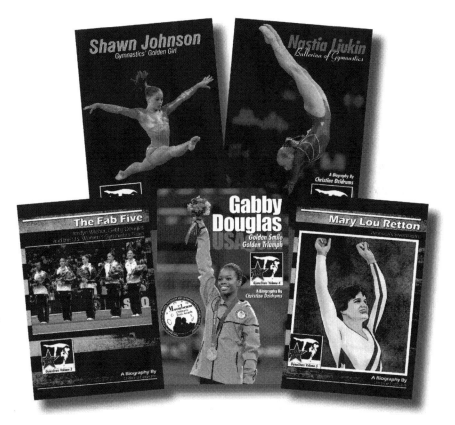

Now sports fans can learn about gymnastics' greatest stars! Americans **Shawn Johnson** and **Nastia Liukin** became the darlings of the 2008 Beijing Olympics when the fearless gymnasts collected 9 medals between them. Four years later at the 2012 London Olympics, America's **Fab Five** claimed gold in the team competition. A few days later, **Gabby Douglas** added another gold medal to her collection when she became the fourth American woman in history to win the Olympic all-around title. The *GymnStars* series reveals these gymnasts' long, arduous path to Olympic glory. *Gabby Douglas: Golden Smile, Golden Triumph* received a **2012 Moonbeam Children's Book Award**.

At the 2010 Vancouver Olympics, tragic circumstances thrust **Joannie Rochette** into the spotlight when her mother died two days before the ladies short program. Joannie then captured hearts everywhere by courageously skating two moving programs to win the Olympic bronze medal. *Joannie Rochette: Canadian Ice Princess* profiles the popular figure skater's moving journey.

Meet figure skating's biggest star: **Yuna Kim**. The Korean trailblazer produced two legendary performances at the 2010 Vancouver Olympic Games to win the gold medal. *Yuna Kim: Ice Queen* uncovers the compelling story of how the beloved figure skater overcame poor training conditions, various injuries and numerous other obstacles to become world and Olympic champion.

Our *YNot Girl* series chronicles the lives and careers of the world's most famous role models. *Jennie Finch: Softball Superstar* details the California native's journey from a shy youngster to softball's most famous face. In *Kelly Clarkson: Behind Her Hazel Eyes*, young readers will find inspiration reading about the superstar's rise from a broke waitress with big dreams to becoming one of the recording industry's top musical acts. *Missy Franklin: Swimming Sensation* narrates the Colorado native's transformation from a talented swimming toddler to queen of the pool.

Theater fans first fell for **Sutton Foster** in her triumphant turn as *Thoroughly Modern Millie*. Since then the triple threat has charmed Broadway audiences by playing a writer, a princess, a movie star, a nightclub singer, and a Transylvania farm girl. Now the two-time Tony winner is conquering television in the acclaimed series *Bunheads*. A children's biography, ***Sutton Foster: Broadway Sweetheart, TV Bunhead*** details the role model's rise from a tiny ballerina to the toast of Broadway and Hollywood.

Idina Menzel's career has been "Defying Gravity" for years! With starring roles in *Wicked* and *Rent*, the Tony-winner is one of theater's most beloved performers. The powerful vocalist has also branched out in other mediums. She has filmed a recurring role on television's smash hit *Glee* and lent her talents to the Disney films, *Enchanted* and *Frozen*. A children's biography, ***Idina Menzel: Broadway Superstar*** narrates the actress' rise to fame from a Long Island wedding singer to overnight success!

SportStars focuses on the world's most successful and influential athletes. ***Matt Kemp: True Blue Baseball Star*** tells the story of one of the Dodgers most successful players in history. ***Mike Trout: Baseball Sensation*** chronicles the New Jersey native's rise from a toddler running the base paths to winning the 2012 American League Rookie of the Year Award. A children's biography, ***66: The Yasiel Puig Story*** will help young readers learn about the man behind the baseball legend. ***Clayton Kershaw: Pitching Ace*** is the latest title in the ***SportsStars Series***!

Future Presidents Club
Girls Rule!

Ashley Moore wants to know why there's never been a girl president. Before long the inspired six-year-old creates a special, girls-only club - the **Future Presidents Club**. Meet five enthusiastic young girls who are ready to change the world. *Future Presidents Club: Girls Rule* is the first book in a series about girls making a difference!

Meet **Princess Dessabelle**, a spoiled, lonely princess with a quick temper.

In *Princess Dessabelle Makes a Friend*, the lonely youngster discovers the meaning of true friendship. *Princess Dessabelle: Tennis Star* finds the pampered girl learning the importance of good sportsmanship.

The SoCal Series

2010 Moonbeam Children's Book Award Winner! In a series of raw journal entries written to her absentee father, a teenager chronicles her penchant for self-harm, a serious struggle with depression and an inability to vocally express her feelings.

"I play the 'What If?'" game all the time. It's a cruel, wicked game."

When free spirit Kaylee suffers a devastating loss, her personality turns dark as she struggles with depression and unresolved anger. Can Kaylee repair her broken spirit, or will she remain a changed person?

Twelve-year-old Emylee Markette has felt invisible her entire life. Then one fateful afternoon, three beautiful sisters arrive in her sleepy New England town and instantly become the most popular girls at Forest Springs Middle School. To everyone's surprise, the Fay sisters befriend Emylee and welcome her into their close-knit circle. Before long, the shy loner finds herself running with the cool crowd, joining the track team and even becoming friends with her lifelong crush.

Through it all, though, Emylee's weighed down by nagging suspicions. Why were the Fay sisters so anxious to befriend her? How do they know some of her inner thoughts? What do they truly want from her?

When Emylee eventually discovers that her new friends are secretly fairies, she finds her life turned upside down yet again and must make some life-changing decisions.

Fair Youth: Emylee of Forest Springs marks the first volume in an exciting new book series.

Made in the USA
Middletown, DE
19 March 2017